Michelle Kwan

by Catherine Goodridge

Table of Contents

Who Is Michelle Kwan?

Michelle Kwan is considered one of the best **figure skaters** of all time. She has **competed** in figure skating events around the world. Michelle has won the U.S. Figure Skating Championships six times. She has also been the world **champion** four times. She has been given more perfect scores from judges than any other skater in history!

▲ Michelle Kwan waves to the crowd after winning a gold medal in the World Figure Skating Championships in 2000.

▲ Michelle was born on July 7, 1980, in California. In this 1994 photograph, Michelle (center) poses with her father and her sister, Karen.

How Did Michelle Become a Figure Skater?

Michelle started skating when she was 5 years old. From early on, she loved to skate. She showed a lot of skill on the ice. She began to dream of being one of the best skaters in the world.

▲ Even as a child, Michelle was determined to be a great figure skater.

In 1992 she started to work with a **coach** named Frank Carroll. He had helped other top skaters train for **national** and **international competitions.** He would help Michelle, too.

▲ Michelle trained with coach Frank Carroll for 10 years.

Michelle placed ninth in her first major competition. She was not happy with this result, but she did not give up. Instead she worked harder. She went to the practice rink earlier and trained longer.

▲ Thirteen-year-old Michelle skates in a competition in Texas in 1993.

Like all skaters, Michelle had to learn many moves. Some of these moves were easy to learn. Others were very hard. To make them all look easy, Michelle had to practice them over and over.

▲ Michelle gets a helping hand during a practice session.

In 1994, when Michelle was only 14, she finished second at the U.S. Figure Skating Championships. That same year she almost made the **Olympic** team.

▲ Michelle performs at the U.S. Figure Skating Championships in 1994.

Although she did not earn a place on the U.S. Olympic team, she got to go to the Games as an alternate skater. If a skater on the U.S. team was not able to compete, Michelle would take her place.

Did You Know?

The Olympic Games started in ancient Greece and were held from 776 B.C. to A.D. 393. They were meant to honor the Greek god Zeus. The modern Olympics began in 1896. They were intended to encourage world peace and friendship.

▲ The interlocking rings on the Olympic flag represent the Americas, Australia, Africa, Asia, and Europe.

Michelle didn't skate at the 1994 Olympic Games, but she watched and learned. She kept practicing very hard. She knew she wanted to skate in the Olympics the next time they were held.

▲ Michelle went to Lillehammer, Norway, for the 1994 Olympic Games.

What Awards Has Michelle Won?

Michelle's hard work paid off. Before long she was winning many competitions. Since 1995 she has not placed lower than third.

▲ Michelle won a gold medal at the 1998 World Figure Skating Championships.

Michelle became one of the best skaters in the world. Many people thought she was the best skater they had ever seen. They said she was like a dancer on the ice.

But there was one competition in which Michelle had failed to take first place. It was the Olympics. Michelle had never won an Olympic gold medal.

In 1998, Michelle skated in the Olympics. She came in second, taking home a silver medal.

Did You Know?

The gold medal winner in the 1998 Games was Tara Lipinski (center). At the age of 15, Tara became the youngest individual gold medal winner in Olympic history.

In 2002, Michelle again went to the Olympics. She had just won the U.S. Figure Skating Championships for the sixth time. Many people believed she would win Olympic gold this time.

▲ Michelle speaks to the press before the 2002 Olympics, in Salt Lake City, Utah.

The Olympic skating competition lasts many days. Michelle was in first place on the final night of the competition. Then, during her final skate, she fell on a jump.

Michelle came in third and won the bronze medal. Although she was very disappointed, she smiled for her fans like the champion she is.

What are Michelle's plans for the future? Whatever she does, she will always be an important part of skating history. She is truly a great figure skater.

Highlights of Michelle Kwan's Career

Year	Event	Result
1994	U.S. Figure Skating Championships	Second place
1996	World Figure Skating Championships	First place
1998	World Figure Skating Championships	First place
	Olympic Games	Second place
2000	World Figure Skating Championships	First place
	U.S. Figure Skating Championships	First place
2001	World Figure Skating Championships	First place
	U.S. Figure Skating Championships	First place
2002	Olympic Games	Third place

Glossary

champion (CHAM-pe-uhn): someone who wins first prize in a contest

coach (KOHCH): a person who trains athletes or teams

compete (kum-PEET): to take part in a contest

competition (kahm-puh-TISH-uhn): a contest or test of skills

figure skater (FIG-yer SKAY-ter): a person who performs athletic and dance moves on ice

international (in-ter-NASH-uh-nul): involving many nations

national (NASH-uh-nul): involving the entire nation

Olympics (oh-LIM-piks): an international contest held every two years

Index